Joseph HAYDN

(1732 – 1809)

Concerto for Piano and Orchestra, Hob. XVIII : 11
D Major / Ré majeur / D-Dur

Piano Reduction

DOWANI International

Preface

This edition presents one of the first concertos that pianists learn to play: Joseph Haydn's Piano Concerto in D Major, Hob. XVIII : 11. Our edition enables you to learn the work systematically at three different tempi, each with a professional accompaniment.

The first CD (CD A) contains the concert version of each movement (piano and orchestra) for you to listen to. When you begin to practice this piece, start at the slow tempo (CD B). If your stereo system is equipped with a balance control, you can place either the solo piano or the piano accompaniment in the foreground by adjusting the control. In the middle position, both pianos can be heard at the same volume. If you do not have a balance control, you can listen to each part on a separate loudspeaker. After you have studied the concerto in the slow tempo, you can advance to the intermediate tempo (CD B) and refine your playing. The piano reduction of the orchestral part at slow and medium tempo is played by a professional coach. Having mastered this practice tempo, you can now advance to the original tempo (CD B) with orchestral accompaniment. At both the middle and original tempi, the piano or orchestral accompaniment can be heard on both channels (without solo piano) in stereo quality. Each movement has been sensibly divided into subsections for practice purposes. You can select the subsection you want using the track numbers indicated in the solo part.

As an aid to ensemble playing with the pianist and the orchestra, the passages where the solo piano plays unaccompanied come with metronome clicks in the background to help you stay in the right tempo. The full cadenzas are only played in the concert version. Each practice tempo gives you time to play a very brief cadenza; you can find the entrance after the cadenza with the aid of the above-mentioned metronome clicks. Further explanations can be found at the end of this volume along with the names of the musicians involved in the recording. More detailed information can be found in the Internet at www.dowani.com. All of the versions were recorded live.

Piano teaching has made enormous progress in recent years. Many piano teachers have their own ideas, theories and experiences, especially in matters of fingering and the use of the pedal. We therefore deliberately refrain from adding fingering or pedaling marks.

We wish you lots of fun playing from our *DOWANI 3 Tempi Play Along* editions and hope that your musicality and diligence will enable you to play the concert version as soon as possible. It is our goal to give you the essential conditions for effective practicing through motivation, enjoyment and fun.

Your DOWANI Team

Avant-propos

Avec cette édition nous vous présentons l'un des premiers concertos pour piano que chaque pianiste apprend à ses début : le concerto pour piano en Ré majeur Hob. XVIII : 11 de Joseph Haydn. Notre édition vous offre la possibilité de travailler l'œuvre d'une manière systématique dans trois différents tempos avec un accompagnement professionnel.

Sur le premier CD (CD A) vous trouverez la version de concert de chaque mouvement (piano et orchestre) pour écouter le morceau. Votre premier contact avec le morceau devrait se faire à un tempo lent (CD B). Si votre chaîne hi-fi dispose d'un réglage de balance, vous pouvez l'utiliser pour mettre au premier plan soit le piano solo, soit l'accompagnement de piano. En équilibrant la balance, vous entendrez les deux pianos à volume égal. Si vous ne disposez pas de réglage de balance, vous entendrez chacun

des pianos sur un des haut-parleurs. Après avoir étudié le morceau à un tempo lent, vous pourrez améliorer votre jeu à un tempo modéré (CD B). La réduction pour piano de la partie d'orchestre sera jouée au tempo lent et au tempo modéré par un répétiteur professionnel. Si vous maîtrisez également ce tempo de travail, vous pourrez jouer le tempo original avec accompagnement d'orchestre (CD B). Dans ces deux tempos – modéré et original – vous entendrez l'accompagnement de piano ou d'orchestre sur les deux canaux en stéréo (sans la partie soliste). Chaque mouvement a été divisé en sections judicieuses pour faciliter le travail. Vous pouvez sélectionner ces sections à l'aide des numéros de plages indiqués dans la partie du soliste. Afin de garantir le meilleur jeu d'ensemble possible avec le répétiteur et l'orchestre et de garder le bon tempo plus facilement, vous entendrez à l'arrière-plan le battement du métronome dans les passages où le piano soliste joue sans accompagnement. Les cadences entières ont été enregistrées seulement dans la version de concert. Aux tempos lent et modéré vous avez le temps de jouer une très brève cadence ; le métronome vous aidera également à trouver l'attaque après la cadence. Pour obtenir plus d'informations et les noms des artistes qui ont participé aux enregistrements, veuillez consulter la dernière page de cette édition ou notre site Internet : www.dowani.com. Toutes les versions ont été enregistrées en direct.

La pédagogie instrumentale pour le piano a beaucoup progressé au cours des dernières années. Beaucoup de professeurs de piano ont leurs propres idées, leurs théories et leurs expériences – surtout en ce qui concerne les doigtés et l'utilisation de la pédale. C'est la raison pour laquelle nous avons délibérément renoncé à indiquer les doigtés et les signes pour la pédale.

Nous vous souhaitons beaucoup de plaisir à faire de la musique avec la collection *DOWANI 3 Tempi Play Along* et nous espérons que votre musicalité et votre application vous amèneront aussi rapidement que possible à la version de concert. Notre but est de vous offrir les bases nécessaires pour un travail efficace par la motivation et le plaisir.

Les Éditions DOWANI

Vorwort

Mit dieser Ausgabe präsentieren wir Ihnen eines der ersten Konzerte, welches man sich als Pianist erarbeitet: das Klavierkonzert in D-Dur Hob. XVIII : 11 von Joseph Haydn. Unsere Ausgabe ermöglicht es Ihnen, das Werk systematisch und in drei verschiedenen Tempi mit professioneller Begleitung zu erarbeiten.

Auf der ersten CD (CD A) finden Sie die Konzertversion eines jeden Satzes (Klavier und Orchester) zum Anhören. Ihr erster Übe-Kontakt mit dem Stück sollte im langsamen Tempo (CD B) stattfinden. Wenn Ihre Stereoanlage über einen Balance-Regler verfügt, können Sie im langsamen Tempo durch Drehen des Reglers entweder das Solo-Klavier oder die Klavierbegleitung stufenlos in den Vordergrund blenden. In der Mittelposition erklingen beide Klaviere gleich laut. Falls Sie keinen Balance-Regler haben, hören Sie jedes Klavier jeweils auf einem Lautsprecher. Nachdem Sie das Stück im langsamen Tempo einstudiert haben, können Sie Ihr Spiel im mittleren Tempo (CD B) verfeinern. Den Klavierauszug des Orchesterparts übernimmt im langsamen und mittleren Tempo ein professioneller Korrepetitor. Wenn Sie auch dieses Übe-Tempo beherrschen, können Sie mit Orchester im originalen Tempo (CD B) musizieren. Die Klavier- bzw. Orchesterbegleitung erklingt im mittleren und originalen Tempo auf beiden Kanälen in Stereo-Qualität (ohne Solo-Klavier). Jeder Satz wurde in sinnvolle Übe-Abschnitte unterteilt. Diese können Sie mit Hilfe der in der Solostimme angegebenen Track-Nummern auswählen. Damit ein optimales Zusammenspiel mit dem Korrepetitor und dem Orchester gewährleistet ist, hören Sie an den Stellen, an denen das Soloklavier ohne Begleitung spielt, als Orientierungshilfe Metronomklicks im Hintergrund, um im richtigen Tempo zu bleiben. Die Kadenzen werden nur in der Konzertversion komplett gespielt. Bei den Übe-Tempi haben Sie jeweils Zeit für eine sehr kurze Kadenz; den Einsatz nach der Kadenz finden Sie mit Hilfe der oben erwähnten Metronomklicks. Weitere Erklärungen sowie die Namen der Künstler finden Sie auf der letzten Seite dieser Ausgabe; ausführlichere Informationen können Sie im Internet unter www.dowani.com nachlesen. Alle eingespielten Versionen wurden live aufgenommen.

Die Klavierpädagogik hat in den letzten Jahren sehr große Fortschritte gemacht. Viele Klavierlehrer haben ihre eigenen Ideen, Theorien und Erfahrungen – vor allem in Bezug auf Fingersätze und die Verwendung des Pedals. Aus diesem Grund haben wir bewusst auf Fingersätze und Pedalanweisungen verzichtet.

Wir wünschen Ihnen viel Spaß beim Musizieren mit unseren *DOWANI 3 Tempi Play Along*-Ausgaben und hoffen, dass Ihre Musikalität und Ihr Fleiß Sie möglichst bald bis zur Konzertversion führen werden. Unser Ziel ist es, Ihnen durch Motivation, Freude und Spaß die notwendigen Voraussetzungen für effektives Üben zu schaffen.

Ihr DOWANI Team

Concerto

for Piano and Orchestra, Hob. XVIII:11
D Major / Ré majeur / D-Dur

J. Haydn (1732 – 1809)

DOW 17005

230

235

Cadenza*

241

II

Joseph HAYDN

(1732 – 1809)

Concerto for Piano and Orchestra, Hob. XVIII : 11
D Major / Ré majeur / D-Dur

Piano / Klavier

DOWANI International

Piano

Concerto
for Piano and Orchestra, Hob. XVIII:11
D Major / Ré majeur / D-Dur

I A1

J. Haydn (1732 – 1809)

9

*Only in concert version   DOW 17005

II

14

III

Rondo all' Ungherese

B8 B19 B30

Allegro assai

16

Minore

Maggiore

B11 **B22** **B33**

Tutti

B7 B18 B29

28

Cadenza*

Piano
Solo

*Only in concert version

DOW 17005

Piano Solo

Piano II

30

III

Rondo all' Ungherese

B9 **B20** **B31**

B10 B21 B32

ENGLISH

DOWANI CD:

- Track numbers in circles
- Track numbers in squares

- slow Play Along Tempo
- intermediate Play Along Tempo
- original Play Along Tempo

- Additional tracks for longer movements or pieces
- **Double CD:** CD1 = A, CD2 = B
- **Concert version:** piano and orchestra
- **Slow tempo:** channel 1: piano solo; channel 2: piano accompaniment; middle position: both pianos at the same volume
- **Intermediate tempo:** piano accompaniment only
- **Original tempo:** orchestra only

Please note that the recorded version of the piano accompaniment may differ slightly from the sheet music. This is due to the spontaneous character of live music making and the artistic freedom of the musicians. The original sheet music for the solo part is, of course, not affected.

Cadenzas: The full cadenzas are only played in the concert version.

FRANÇAIS

DOWANI CD :

- N° de plage dans un cercle
- N° de plage dans un rectangle

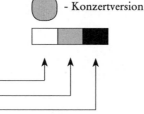

- tempo lent play along
- tempo moyen play along
- tempo original play along

- Plages supplémentaires pour mouvements ou morceaux longs
- **Double CD :** CD1 = A, CD2 = B
- **Version de concert :** piano et orchestre
- **Tempo lent :** 1er canal : piano solo ; 2nd canal : accompagnement de piano ; au milieu : les deux pianos au même volume
- **Tempo moyen :** seulement l'accompagnement de piano
- **Tempo original :** seulement l'accompagnement d'orchestre

L'enregistrement de l'accompagnement de piano peut présenter quelques différences mineures par rapport au texte de la partition. Ceci est du à la liberté artistique des musiciens et résulte d'un jeu spontané et vivant, mais n'affecte, bien entendu, d'aucune manière la partie soliste.

Cadences : Les cadences entières ont été enregistrées seulement dans la version de concert.

DEUTSCH

DOWANI CD:

- Trackangabe im Kreis
- Trackangabe im Rechteck

- langsames Play Along Tempo
- mittleres Play Along Tempo
- originales Play Along Tempo

- Zusätzliche Tracks bei längeren Sätzen oder Stücken
- **Doppel-CD:** CD1 = A, CD2 = B
- **Konzertversion:** Klavier und Orchester
- **Langsames Tempo:** 1. Kanal: Klavier solo; 2. Kanal: Klavierbegleitung; Mitte: beide Klaviere in gleicher Lautstärke
- **Mittleres Tempo:** nur Klavierbegleitung
- **Originaltempo:** nur Orchester

Die Klavierbegleitung auf der CD-Aufnahme kann gegenüber dem Notentext kleine Abweichungen aufweisen. Dies geht in der Regel auf die künstlerische Freiheit der Musiker und auf spontanes, lebendiges Musizieren zurück. Die Solostimme bleibt davon selbstverständlich unangetastet.

Kadenzen: Die Kadenzen sind nur in der Konzertversion komplett eingespielt.

DOWANI - 3 Tempi Play Along is published by:
DOWANI International
A division of De Haske (International) AG
Postfach 60, CH-6332 Hagendorn,
Switzerland
Phone: +41-(0)41-785 82 50 / Fax +41-(0)41-785 82 58
Email: info@dowani.com
www.dowani.com

Recording & Digital Mastering: Pavel Lavrenenkov, Russia
Music Notation: Notensatz Thomas Metzinger, Germany
Design: Andreas Haselwanter, Austria

Concert Version
Vedrana Kovac, Piano
Russian Philharmonic Orchestra Moscow
Konstantin Krimets, Conductor

3 Tempi Accompaniment
Slow:
Vedrana Kovac, Piano

Intermediate:
Vedrana Kovac, Piano

Original:
Russian Philharmonic Orchestra Moscow
Konstantin Krimets, Conductor